"Men hang out signs indicative of their
respective trades; Shoemakers hang out a gigantic shoe;
Jewelers, a monster watch; and the Dentist hangs out a gold tooth;
But up in the mountains of New Hampshire,
God Almighty has hung out a sign to show
that there He makes men."

Daniel Webster

NEW HAMPSHIRE

A Scenic Discovery

Photographs & Introduction: Clyde H. Smith

Published by Foremost Publishers, Inc.

Recollections of the Granite State

It was April 12, 1934 when New Hampshire's Mt. Washington recorded an event unparalleled in the history of meteorology – the highest natural wind ever observed on the face of our planet! The summit Weather Observatory, in its infancy then, measured an incredible gust of 231 miles per hour . . . just before its anemometer blew away.

With all the mighty mountains in the world it seems incongruous that tiny New Hampshire should have the title, but the record wind on New England's highest peak stands to this day.

I can still remember when I first climbed Mt. Washington with my parents. I was four years old. My father worked for the Forest Service and took me everywhere as soon as I could walk. I remember gripping lichen-covered rocks with my sneakers while ascending the famous Tuckerman Ravine Trail. It was early summer and skiers schussed down Tuckerman's great snow bowl where the last vestiges of winter still remained longer than any other place in the East.

Above the ravine's headwall, Washington's exposed summit loomed like a gigantic rockpile. At four years, my short legs could barely scramble up over those slippery boulders. My sneakers were always coming untied and I kept tripping over my laces. To make matters worse the wind got stronger and I was buffeted about like a ping-pong ball. My parents tried to help, but even they had to cling to the rocks. At the summit, we found shelter in a stone building called the Tip Top House. Built in 1854, it has remained as America's oldest mountain-top dwelling.

New Hampshire's mountains were the foundations of my youth and one in particular, Mt. Cardigan, became my home for nine years. My father was assigned there as a fire lookout warden. We lived in a small one-room cabin just a short distance from the fire tower. In the summer, swarms of people came up from the valleys to pick wild berries. My mother and I would also scour the mountain for wild berries. We used to sell them at the summer resorts in nearby Canaan. (Mom had many secret places where she was able to avoid the crowds that invaded Cardigan's berry patches.)

The delicious berries also attracted other natives – black bears. On one occasion, Mom watched from a cliff while I picked berries on one side of an island of bushes, and a big black bear munched away on the other side. The bear was near my mother, so she dared not call out for fear the bear would run diagonally across the patch towards me. Eventually, the bear worked its way around to one side while I kept picking on the opposite, each oblivious of the other!

Wildlife was always a part of my early childhood on Mt. Cardigan. It was common to see wildcats, lynx, bears, deer, foxes and many other animals. In all my encounters, I was never threatened or intimidated by any wild creature. I was taught there were times to respect an animal's right of way, such as when a mother bear came strolling by with her cubs. Porcupines were also quite common and delighted in chewing discarded boxes. At night, they would squeal outside our cabin, calling all their relatives to dinner. When they started gnawing down our outhouse, my father took exception and declared war on the critters.

Wild thunderstorms often hit the mountain with ear-splitting force. Several times during those years, the tower was demolished by lightning. I vividly remember a bolt out of the blue coming in through our cabin telephone line, dancing around the room, then grounding out on our iron cooking stove. It was accompanied by a deafening thunderclap that left our ears ringing for days. Sometimes we would stand outside our cabin and watch storms approach from the distance. There was so much static electricity that my parents' hair would stand straight up. I suppose mine did too, but it might have been more from fright than from electricity.

We survived the great hurricane of 1938 in our tiny cabin. Enormous chains circled the roof, and were anchored to the ledges with iron pins. These were used to protect the cabin from howling winter storms. During the '38 hurricane, we huddled inside listening to our radio crackle out news of the impending destruction just minutes before it hit. We surely would have been blown off the mountain if it hadn't been for those chains. All during that terrible night, we could feel the cabin lifting up and down on its foundation, while the chains clanked and strained with frightful noise. In the morning, trees were uprooted all around, and the forest was completely flattened.

We did not live on the mountain in winter. There was no fire danger then of course, so the lookout's job was suspended until spring. We were back on top by April, and even though the valleys were turning green, there was still plenty of snow around. During this time, I had the most difficulty going to school. I had to hike 3½ miles each way, rain or shine. In the spring, I used snowshoes. It seemed easy enough but spring snow conditions were unstable. My snowshoes would fall through unseen pockets and at times, I had to flounder in snow up to my hips. I was soaking wet by the time I reached school and exhausted by the time I reached home, sometimes after dark.

Over the ensuing years, I made many trips to Mt. Washington and its Presidential Range, as well as the Franconia Range, Mahoosucs, Chocorua, Pemigewasset Wilderness and countless other places. Gone were the sneakers from my first hike and in their place I acquired a pair of "Limmers" made by Peter Limmer of Intervale, NH. (Limmer boots are world famous and are quite possibly the best all-around hiking/climbing boots ever made.)

In the early 1960's, I began winter mountaineering on many of my old familiar haunts, pioneering the use of igloos for shelters above the timberline. Mt. Washington was always my nemesis with its high winds. Once, a group I was leading became marooned near the summit. For four days, we were confined to our igloos during a wild storm. At times, the wind peaked to 121 miles per hour and once, sustained 100 miles per hour for 18 hours straight. The temperature dropped to 30° below zero. (We learned these statistics from the Weather Observatory much later.) The wind was so strong, it was impossible to stand. Breathing was a struggle because the wind compressed against our bodies and appeared to suck the air away before we could take it in. Our igloos saved us but the scouring snow worked on them like a buzz saw, so we had to continually build secondary walls with snowblocks to prevent the main shelter from being eaten away. By using our heads, our hands and the right equipment, we were able to survive Mt. Washington's harsh weather. Four days later, we walked off under our own power. Many people have not been so lucky. In fact, more than 100 fatalities have occurred on the mountain since 1849. And New England's highest peak has earned the dubious distinction of having the "worst weather in the world".

Although it has been the state's rugged White Mountains that I remember most, I became familiar with other places, too. In all, I like to think of the Granite State in terms of six, maybe even seven distinct regions: *The Seacoast,* (shortest in the nation) – eighteen miles of sweeping sandy beaches crowned with Portsmouth's bustling harbor, quaint shops and historic homes. *The Lakes Region,* blessed with incomparable scenery and pristine waters. Island-flecked Winnipesaukee, Winnisquam, Newfound, Ossipee, Squam and Merrymeeting sparkle like a collage of jewels among low-lying hills and rounded mountains. *The White Mountains,* perhaps the state's leading attraction. Here, hundreds of thousands of visitors migrate annually to participate in everything from white water canoeing to watching the foliage turn. *The Dartmouth-Lake Sunapee Region,* features one of the oldest colleges in the country, and lies along the mighty Connecticut River that borders Vermont. *The Monadnock Region,* known as the state's quiet corner where picturesque villages are connected by winding country roads. *The Merrimack Region,* is the industrial belt and contains the state's largest cities and towns, including Concord, Manchester, Nashua and Salem. Finally, there is the remote *Connecticut Lakes Region,* headwaters for the great Connecticut River that empties into Long Island Sound. This is New Hampshire's Wilderness region, a network of winding streams, beaver ponds, and acres upon acres of softwood forests.

For more than fifty years, New Hampshire has been my heritage and my home. In many ways, both the images in this book, and the spirit behind them, were molded by those early days, scampering over granite ledges in my rag-a-muffin sneakers. Yet this collection would not be complete without a word of appreciation to my parents. They instilled in me the resourcefulness so often missing in today's fast-moving world. And so, I dedicate this book to one of the most resourceful people I ever knew, my mother, Hilda Smith, who presented me with my first breath of New Hampshire air.

Clyde H. Smith

Reflections at Chocorua

Nature's paintbrush at work

Canoeing along the Androscoggin

Autumn looks down on Jefferson Meadows

Upward and onward, goes the Cog Railway, Mt. Washington   The Old Man of the Mountain, Franconia Notch

Town Hall, Washington

Snowfall in New Boston

Last chance before the storm, New Boston

A waterfall cuts its way down the mountain   Stark Village on the Upper Ammonoosuc River

Covered bridge spans time and the Ammonoosuc River, Bath

Portsmouth Waterfront   *Overleaf*: Dawn greets fog blanket, Portsmouth Harbor

Harvesting the bounty of the sea, Portsmouth State Fishing Pier

Portrait of a fisherman, Portsmouth

Season's greetings from Whitefield

Nightfall at Portsmouth Harbor

Angry surf at Hampton Beach

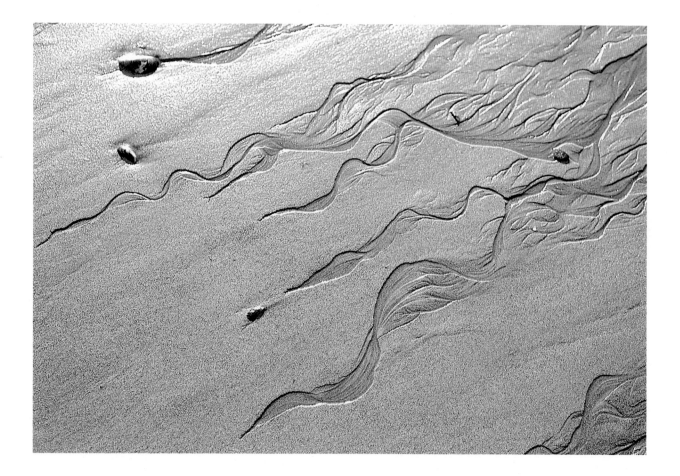

Nature's scrollwork, at Hampton Beach

Scenic notch from the Sanguinary Ridge Trail

A white-tailed deer at home near Connecticut Lake

Squam Lake greenery

Beaverbrook Falls, Colebrook

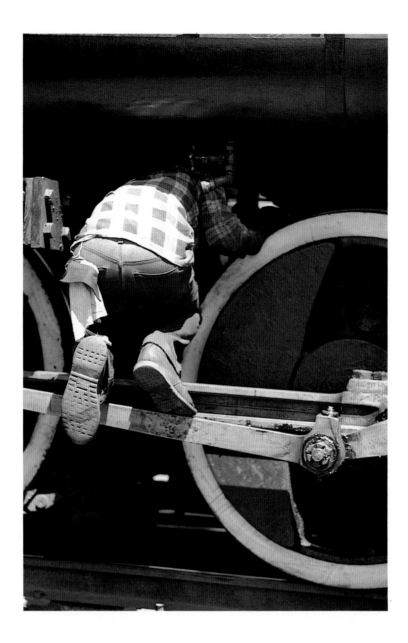

Oiling the drivewheels

Exploring the train station, North Conway

Mt. Lafayette and Franconia Range from Sugar Hill

Up from the water, Connecticut Lake

A study in solitude, Newfound Lake

Cruising along Lake Winnipesaukee

Overleaf: Reflections of Chocorua Lake

Take your pick at Dixville Notch

The Basin at high water, Franconia Notch

Sunset in the pines

Streams of light along the Upper Saco River

Lobster pots waiting for spring

Frigid morning in Portsmouth Harbor

A study in serenity, Franconia

Ice cold motor at Seabrook Harbor

Portsmouth Harbor sunrise

On the Appalachian Trail, Mt. Washington

Tip Top House, Mt. Washington summit

Overleaf: Chugging up Mt. Washington

Linnea Phillips, Summer's child Linnea's field

A picture-perfect day at Stratford

The grandeur of Mount Liberty

Stormy Mount Monroe and the Southern Presidential Range   30° below at Surry

A sea of beach stones, Wallis Sands

Pleasure craft dot a New Hampshire harbor

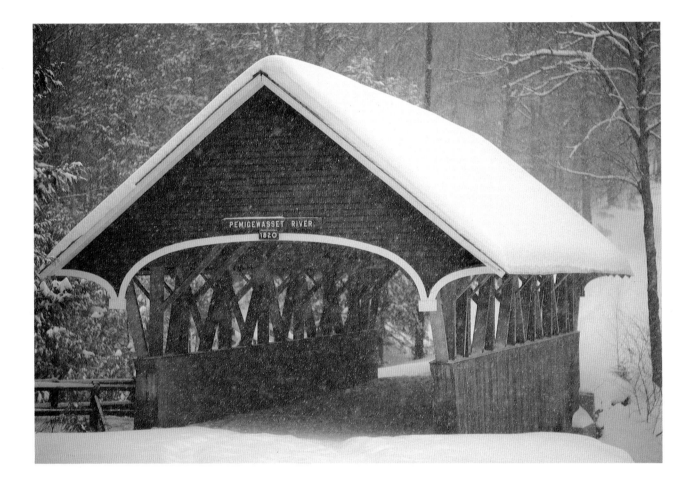

Cross country trail at Sugar Hill   Covered bridge over the Pemigewasset River

Mt. Washington from above the clouds

Waking up to winter, Walpole   *Overleaf:* Autumn's glow in New Hampshire

Proclaiming liberty throughout the land, Concord

Between classes at Dartmouth College

A Tamworth pastoral

Barnstormer's Playhouse Decoration, Tamworth

A snow-swollen stream winds its way home　　　　　Checking the load at New Boston

Summer breezes cool New Castle

A guardian at Isles of Shoals

icy diamonds cling to autumn leaves   The Balsams Resort, Dixville Notch

A weatherbeaten house dries out in the sun

George Roberts and friend, Chocorua

Overleaf: Stark Village Pastoral

A bird's eye view of Wolfeboro on Lake Winnepesaukee

Overlooking Franconia Notch . . . and everything else

ebruary thaw on the Gale River, Franconia   Shaker Village near Canterbury

Letting the chips fly near Pittsburg

Run through Dixville Notch

Flowers welcome you to Madison's Town Hall

Where memories live, Chocorua

Golden view from New Castle